Yorkshire Past

West Riding

Written and compiled by
Stephen Tyndale-Biscoe

at heart ♥ publications

YORKSHIRE POST

First published in 2007 by:
At Heart Ltd, 32 Stamford Street,
Altrincham, Cheshire, WA14 1EY
in conjunction with
Yorkshire Post Newspapers Ltd
PO Box 168, Wellington Street,
Leeds, LS1 1RF

ISBN: 978-1-84547-127-9

Printed and bound by Bell & Bain Ltd, Glasgow

Introduction

Industry is synonymous with the towns and cities of
West Yorkshire. The archive photos on the pages of
this book capture that sense of industry which sweeps
across a swathe of Northern England, making it utterly
distinctive. But while its story since the turn of the 20th
century has included industrial growth and decline, it
has also seen astonishing changes in transport. As car
ownership, once restricted to the wealthy, boomed so
that nearly-empty streets became swamped by cars,
public transport moved in the course of 60 years from
horse-drawn, via trams and then trolley-buses, to recent
ancestors of the buses we see on the streets today. Of
all these forms, trams had the greatest visual impact,
and the extent to which they dominated the urban
landscape is seen in many of these pictures. They seem
to show another world, yet in it are the seeds of a great
deal that is familiar today.

Written and compiled by Stephen Tyndale-Biscoe, 2007

Spring

• Wakefield Cattle Market. The market
was moved to George Street in 1765,
and in the 1800s it was the biggest cattle
market in northern England. It was sold
to Wakefield Corporation in 1938 and
it finally closed in 1965.

● A picturesque corner of Heptonstall, April 2, 1964. The date above the arch is 1578, however some parts of the village date back to 100 AD.

● Coley Church, near Northowram, as much in the middle of nowhere today as it was when this photo was taken on March 30, 1914.

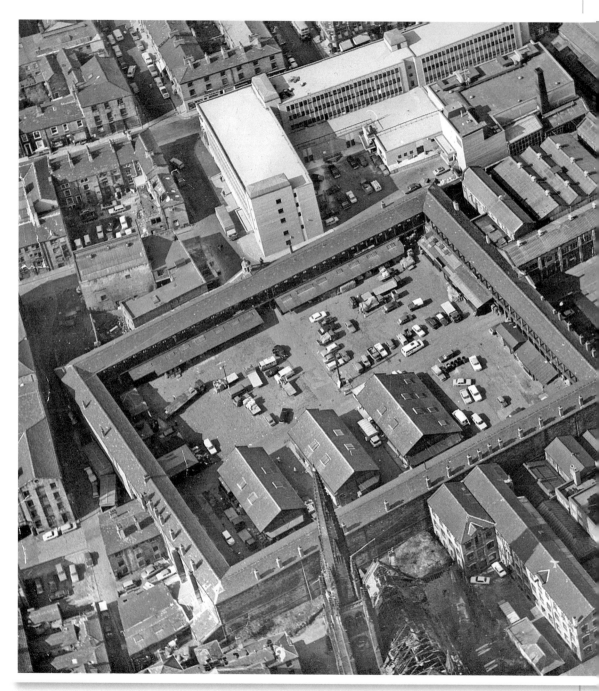

• Aerial view of the Piece Hall at Halifax, April 1973, years before its potential as a tourist attraction was recognised.

● Some of the new police mini-vans recently delivered to Police Headquarters, Wakefield, all neatly lined up for a photo call on April 29, 1967.

• May 1971 and Eric, an inmate at Wakefield Prison, shows off some of the tropical fish he had bred during his sentence.

• Wakefield Bull Ring, 1949. In 2007 it was at the heart of a £175m refurbishment scheme.

● A bus conductress in 1956, looking improbably well
turned out, the Leeds City crest on her cap badge.

Trams in Cookridge Street, with St Anne's Cathedral on the right, in 1946.

● A state-of-the-art tram in post-war Leeds, looking down Wellington Street past the Majestic (which later became the Majestyk Club).

● Somethings do change. City
Square, Leeds, when trams were
the main form of public transport
in the city.

● Seamstresses working at David Little and
Co. Ltd, Water Lane, Holbeck, Leeds, when
clothes were made in England, May 16, 1968.

● Bolton Brow Methodist Church on the main road in Sowerby Bridge had been given a facelift when this picture was taken on April 2, 1970. "It is a good example of how a cleaned-up church should look", said Mr. Mark Andrew, Director of the Yorkshire and Humberside Clean-up Campaign.

● Aerial view of Bradford looking south-west, the cathedral in the centre foreground and the Town Hall left of centre at the top, in May 1959.

● Whit Walk photographed at the tram terminus, Thornhill, in 1905. A reminder of the importance attached to Whitsuntide, which has declined over the last 50 years to the point at which it is barely noted today.

• A snowy April 1st in St George's Square, Huddersfield in 1938. A Rolls Royce is parked opposite the St George's Hotel.

• A substantial mill fire in Brighouse, May 1905, attracts a large crowd of on-lookers, many of whom are watching their jobs go up in smoke.

Summer

● Lunchtime break in Forster Square,
Bradford, on a warm June day in 1957.

● Brighouse Mayoral
Parade, 1923.

● The beginning of a sad ending
as demolition work began on
the Palace Theatre, Halifax, in
1958. The theatre, also known
as the Palace Hippodrome, was
built in 1903 by Runtz and Ford.

• In 1973 Dynamite Delaney was at work in Halifax, where he and his men were making parts of Square Chapel safer; with a nudge from a 3-ton ball suspended from a jib on a crane, tons of tottering masonry came crashing to the ground. The Chapel, extraordinary for being a square, brick building in a town of stone, was constructed in 1772 and designed by the then 18-year-old Thomas Bradley, who is also thought to have designed the Piece Hall. Calderdale Council acquired the disused building in 1969 and were soon seeking permission to demolish it. Despite being a Grade II Listed Building, the Square Chapel remained seriously threatened until 1988 when it was bought by the Square Chapel Trust which set about making it safe and then restoring it. The Square Chapel then began a new lease of life as a thriving arts centre.

● St Matthew's Church garden party, in Rastrick, 1966. The VIPs are a couple of rows back, sporting pearls, expensive outfits and hats. But not everyone's attention is on the Vicar.

● An aerial view of Huddersfield looking north on August 17, 1953. Longley Park Golf Club in the foreground and behind it the Huddersfield Broad Canal which runs between the Huddersfield Narrow Canal in the centre of Huddersfield, to the Calder and Hebble Navigation at Cooper Bridge. At one time it was known as Sir John Ramsden's Canal, after the Lord of the manor and main landowner. It later became known as the Broad Canal to distinguish it from the Narrow Canal. It was opened in 1776 and proved to be a lifeline for the rapidly developing textile industry in Huddersfield, bringing in coal and shipping out finished textiles. Perhaps the most interesting feature on the canal is the lift bridge at Quay Street, Huddersfield. Until recently this was windlass-operated although it is now electric. Despite being a lift bridge it is known as Turnbridge. The bridge is also known as Locomotive Bridge, perhaps due to its similarity to early steam locomotives.

● Huddersfield Market Place, July 1, 1957.

• St George's Square, July 1, 1957, with its blackened buildings including the railway station on the far side and the George Hotel on the right. In 1895 the Rugby League was formed at a meeting in the hotel.

● Cloth Hall Street, Huddersfield, on July 1, 1957. The Hillman van in the centre was a popular workhorse. On the right is a Jowett Javelin, the car that was built in Bradford, and beyond it a Vauxhall Wyvern, the most American-looking British-built car of the 1950s.

• Train spotters get as close to the end of the platform as they can to watch *The Welsh Guardsman* 4-6-0 locomotive as it pauses outside Leeds City Station in the summer of 1958.

• Leeds in 1947, the traffic lights where Bond Street meets Park Row were the first of their kind in the country.

● Near Royal Park Horticultural Gardens, the Tam O'Shanter Tram.

● Wakefield Jail, July 14, 1974. The new entrance to Wakefield Prison, the unbelievable winner of the bronze plaque as "best in the public section" of an architectural awards scheme. The mind boggles at what its rivals must have been like, but in 1974 such monstrous carbuncles were springing up all over the place and attracting much praise from official bodies, while the public hurried by with averted eyes.

• Six Chimneys, Lower Kirkgate in the 19th century. The building fell down in 1941 and at first a German bomb was blamed, but as it turned out the building collapsed because an inside supporting wall had been removed.

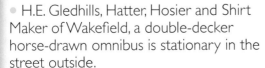
• H.E. Gledhills, Hatter, Hosier and Shirt Maker of Wakefield, a double-decker horse-drawn omnibus is stationary in the street outside.

• The junction of Warrengate and the Springs, Wakefield, around 1890.

● A steam tug pulls an articulated train of some 17 coal-carrying units on the River Aire Canal at Allerton Bywater in June 1955, when 'King Coal' reigned supreme.

● Boar Lane, Leeds, early 20th century. The fine buildings on the left were all doomed and would be gone by the end of that century.

• Six minutes past 12 noon in Briggate, Leeds, late 19th century, and all was hustle and bustle. At least that hasn't changed.

Briggate, Leeds,
early 20th century.

• Midday in Briggate, Leeds. The horse-drawn vehicles of a few years earlier have gone - in their place, tram lines and a motor car.

● Great excitement at the opening of Guiseley's tramway on June 30, 1909.

● Gathering of the Love (and drugs) Generation
in Potternewton Park, Leeds, on July 10, 1971.

● Brook Street, Ilkley. This picture was taken the
day after the iron railway bridge was removed.

• Hay harvest at Sam Moss' farm, Wood Nook, Pudsey.

The site of the Merrion Centre, Leeds, 1945, showing the great fire-fighting water tank created to fight a blitz on the city that never came. None of the buildings in this view would survive many years more, as the face of Leeds was transformed.

Pudsey parade,
early 20th century.

The Leeds-Liverpool Canal
at Rodley, summer 1934.

• From the top of Rawdon Billing, which rises to 750ft looking over Larkfield Dam.

• View near Chapel Allerton from Stainbeck Lane.

• Leeds, June 22, 1981. This picture taken from the tower of St John's Church in the centre of Leeds shows office workers taking in the sun during their lunch break.

● Yeadon Airport, June 1957, an aerial view of Yeadon
Aerodrome – later to be known as Leeds-Bradford Airport.

Yeadon Yacht Dinghy Race, Yeadon Moor Dam in August 1955.

• Dignitaries line up for the opening of Hipperholme Town Hall on August 13, 1899.

• Fish friers and fish merchants operating in the famous Halifax Piece Hall in the 1920s, already a scruffy ghost of what it had once been, with sacks draped over the second-floor railings and the ground floor stone work hidden behind lean-to sheds.

The Piece Hall in Halifax in the summer of 1969.
It was so badly regarded that someone attached a
washing line to an entrance support.

Three generations of housing at Halifax in the summer of 1965. In the foreground the old Grindlestone Bank Farm, in the background traditional post-war homes on the Bankedge estate and centre, the six blocks of flats at Jumples, Mixenden. The first of the flats was opened by Councillor Harry Ludlam, Mayor of Halifax, a few days after this picture was taken.

Halifax, Piece Hall, as seen on July 21, 1971. No one imagined then that it could ever become a tourist attraction and performance space.

A tram trundles through the cobbled streets of Halifax at the turn of the century.

Wainhouse Tower, 1947. This distinctive landmark was built as a chimney to disperse smoke from dye works, owned by John Edward Wainhouse, lower down the hill. He wanted it to have architectural merit, and it acquired rather more than he originally intended when its role as a chimney ended before it began. Wainhouse finished it off as a tower, with a cupola on the top with two galleries around the outside. Completed in 1875, the 253ft structure had taken four years to build.

• A picture of pure bliss on the Leeds-Liverpool
Canal at Apperley Bridge on a sunny July day in
1951.

Whatever occurred here in Bradford on July 30, 1907 caused a great deal of mess and a great deal of interest. The tram on its side appears to have lost its top deck.

A loom at Scott Textiles, Bradford, on July 29, 1954,
when Bradford's textile industries were still flourishing.

• A common enough sight in Bradford in 1954 - this photo of the spinning shed of Scott Textiles was taken on July 29 - but over the coming decades it would become increasingly rare. Not only are rather few spinning sheds left, but their minders would no doubt be wearing ear defenders as protection against the deafening clatter - and especially when posing for a newspaper photographer.

Autumn

• Dewsbury vs Batley, Crown Flatt. September 28, 1912, and players run onto the pitch at the start of the Rugby League local derby, watched by the cream of the two towns' society, sitting on the front row. The stadium was destroyed by arsonists on September 13, 1988.

The new Halifax inner ring road gradually takes shape in 1973.

● A few weeks later and considerable progress on the construction of the new road is plainly visible.

● October 12, 1974. Construction of the Lee Bank flyover, Halifax.

● Wakefield's Olympia Roller Skating Rink in 1909, when roller-skating was all the rage and rinks were appearing in towns and cities up and down the country. Some corporations created temporary rinks by boarding over public swimming pools.

An interior view of the newly-opened extension
at Harry Ramsdens, Guiseley, in 1968.

Leeds tramcars 331, 230 and 22 in Duncan Street, 1936.

The Leeds-Liverpool Canal at Rodley,
on a warm October day, 1950.

● Mr Currer Briggs and his car with registration plate number U1. Mr Briggs was the Lord Mayor of Leeds at the start of the 1900s.

Round House Inn, Halifax, October 15, 1928.

Pity the poor driver of the Number 58 bus, seen here in Baildon in September 1957, or whoever had occasion to try starting it with a starting handle - the hole for which can be seen in the radiator.

A study in determination. Wakefield Trinity, October 1946.

Flooded Royd Street, in Brighouse, photographed on November 4, 1946. A rowing boat is in the distance, but is heading the wrong way to rescue the lorry driver.

Halifax from the South East, on the night of November 22, 1955.

● Artistic shot of the much-photographed Castle Hill Victoria
Tower, Huddersfield, taken on November 9, 1966.

● Heavy vehicles nose to tail on the A62 Huddersfield-Manchester Road at Standedge on November 13, 1959. A reminder of what users of the trans-Pennine main road had to put up with before the construction of the M62.

● November 27, 1958. A gas flare was brought into use in City Square, Leeds, to illuminate the traffic policeman on duty in the fog.

● Town Hall Square, Bradford, on November 15, 1956, before the wholesale demolitions began which turned parts of the city centre into a by-word for officially-sanctioned urban vandalism.

• Panorama from the clock tower of Bradford Town Hall, photographed on the same sunny November day.

• Looking towards Lockwood in November 1945. Calder
Canal is in the foreground.

Looking west to Golcar. Crowther's Mill is in the foreground.

Winter

● Glasshoughton Colliery, February 7, 1938. Although surface coal had been taken from round about Glasshoughton for over 200 years, it was not until 1793 that a coal mine was founded there. The colliery finally closed in 1986.

● February 7, 1938, and changing shifts at Glasshoughton Collieries met on the footbridge over the railway that carried away the hard-won coal. The two at the bottom of the stairs are carrying safety lamps.

The opening ceremony of the County Hall, Wakefield, on February 21, 1890, the top-hatted dignitaries in a flower-bedecked gazebo.

This post box of the sort usually embedded in a pre-existing wall has its own purpose-built pillar - a handsome one, too - but this peculiarity did not endear itself to Mr Stanley Shaw, aged 78, of Birchen Avenue, Ossett. He considered it to be such a nuisance that he petitioned to have it removed and is pictured looking at it somewhat balefully in this photo taken on December 31, 1968.

● Gary Cooper, Wakefield Trinity full-back, playing in February 1967. An opponent has just performed an ungainly-looking manoeuver, but it didn't stop Mr Cooper who is about to drop over the line.

● Grid-lock 1960s style. This traffic jam in King Cross Street, Halifax, was photographed on February 6, 1963. Two of the lorries have their grills partially blocked to keep their engines warm on a cold winter's day.

● King Cross, Halifax, in a bitter winter in the 1940s. The lorry stacked high with bales of shoddy approaching the men attacking the packed icy snow with picks and shovels looks decidedly unsteady.

March 1963 - The Shay football ground was the
first in the country to be opened up for ice-skating.

● Hand signalman Jack Smith sounded his horn to warn workmen in Standedge railway tunnel in February 1966, of an oncoming train. The tunnel passed under the Pennines and was opened on August 1, 1849. At 3 miles in length, the single-track tunnel was the longest in the world at that time.

● Night scene, 1936. Picture taken from Pinfold, Manchester
Road, Huddersfield, showing Milnsbridge and Longwood, with
John Crowther's Mill in the foreground.

● Looking towards Lindley and taken from Manchester Road. Crowther's Mill is in the foreground. February 6, 1936.

• Swing bridge, with its helpful stop sign, over the Leeds - Liverpool
Canal at Apperley Bridge, February 19, 1968.

• December 1967. Chris Leak, on the left, is pictured as he splashes
along the flooded Castleford-Hook Moor Road at Allerton Bywater
in an attempt to keep the traffic moving. Shortly afterwards the road
became impassable.

An overturned tram on a snowy day outside the Parkinson Building, Leeds University, February 1951. A Standard Vanguard, distinguished with its rounded rear, is just disappearing out of view.

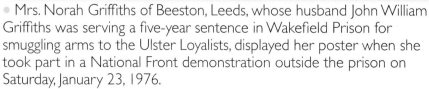

● Mrs. Norah Griffiths of Beeston, Leeds, whose husband John William Griffiths was serving a five-year sentence in Wakefield Prison for smuggling arms to the Ulster Loyalists, displayed her poster when she took part in a National Front demonstration outside the prison on Saturday, January 23, 1976.

• The day after the National Front demonstration outside Wakefield Prison on behalf of jailed Loyalist supporter John Griffiths, members of the Sinn Fein Provisionals (Midland branch) arrived to show their support for two IRA prisoners who were on hunger strike in the jail.

● January 25, 1976. IRA prisoners
on the roof of Wakefield jail.

● Observed by a small number of
very keen-eyed spectators, Wakefield
prisoners meet Ossett Methodists in
a cup-tie at the Ossett Town ground
on December 27, 1969.

● An innovation in 1969 was this "open plan" bus shelter at the junction of Dewsbury Road and the Ring Road, Beeston. The pair pictured waiting for their bus might not have been very impressed, especially on this cold, wet winter's day.

● Mid-winter's day has just past and shadows are stretched by a
bright midday sun in Briggate, Leeds, on December 23, 1959.

January 26, 1938. An aerial view of the vast Lister's Mill, Bradford, on a bright winter's day.

Where Bradford meets Queensbury, on a snowy day in the winter of 1953.

● Rail crash in Dryden Street, Bradford, November 10, 1964. The 15ton steam locomotive and tender of a runaway goods train which plunged more than 30ft into a Bradford street set engineers a recovery problem.

• The building which Bradford YMCA occupied at the junction of Canal Road and Bolton Road was lucky to remain intact when a neighbouring warehouse caught fire in the early 1950s. An aerial shot captured the dramatic scene.

• January 23, 1964. Seamstresses making skirts in the sewing room of A. Riddell & Co. Ltd, wholesale gown and mantle manufacturers, Bradford.

One of the wrecked lighting gantries at Bradford Park Avenue football ground following the gales on February 11, 1962. A second can be seen at the far end of the stand.